ADVENTURES IN EROTICISM: *FOUR SEASONS*

By: Immani Love

Adventures in Eroticism: Four Seasons
By: Immani Love

Printed in the United States of America
First Printing, 2011

ISBN 978-1-257-65370-6

www.ImmaniLove.com

Table of Contents

Intro: *"Don't judge a book by its cover"*

One thing people always tell me is *"NEVER JUDGE A BOOK BY ITS COVER."* There are people out there that are not what they seem. Like books in a library, you pick it up and the title says one thing but the book itself is something totally different.

We've all met them, like the hardback book, *"Thug Life,"* the thug Stud, hard, dresses like a dude, hair cut low, treats her woman like her trophy. But get in her in the bedroom finger her the right way for an hour or two and she's screams and cries like a femme. Hardback book?

How about the classic, *"Little Women,"* a prissy little femme, 5'2, 110lbs, quiet, tiny voice, gentle and wouldn't hurt a fly. But get her alone and she straps up and hits it from the back like a jockey. Classic novel?

"The Wall Street Journal," the banker, she wears three piece suits, expensive jewelry, frequents the finest restaurants, and drives the best cars. She said she want a hood nigga...only dates down ass bitches, the hoes with bullet holes and stab wounds. Financial Periodical?

"Swan Lake," the Ballerina, who's slender, graceful, well-trained, limber body has been climbing poles, gyrating on stage and dancing for three years. Lap dances are her specialty with one leg behind her head. Ballet at its best.

Then there's the romance novel, Immani Love, statuesque, eloquent, professional demeanor, introvert. She will freak your body in ways that can only be described in the most erotic foreign films, dare you to tell your friends because they're next on the list while you wish for your next moment alone with her. Then she'll write a poem about you and read it to the masses. Adventures in Eroticism.

Maybe you can judge a book by its cover.

Spring Escapades: *Step by Step*

Talk to me , she says... Tell me what you're gonna do to me...I look at her...mentally running through the scenarios in my head. Ok, wait a minute. Close your eyes and listen carefully. Let me give it to you step by step...

Step 1- Blindfold you- I want you to feel everything I do.

Step 2- Massage your body from head to toe...letting my hands roam every inch of your body...from your scalp to your fingertips to your pinky toes. Don't my hands feel good?

Step 3 - Use my favorite condiments to decorate your body...let's see...there's the whipped cream on your nipples, the chocolate syrup down the front of your chest drawing an arrow to your pussy, the pudding cupped in your pelvic cavity, the cherries between each toe... pop rocks and ice by the bed...I'm an artist aren't I? Take my time and eat you slowly, start at the toes and work my way up. Dayum! My desert was finger-licking good!

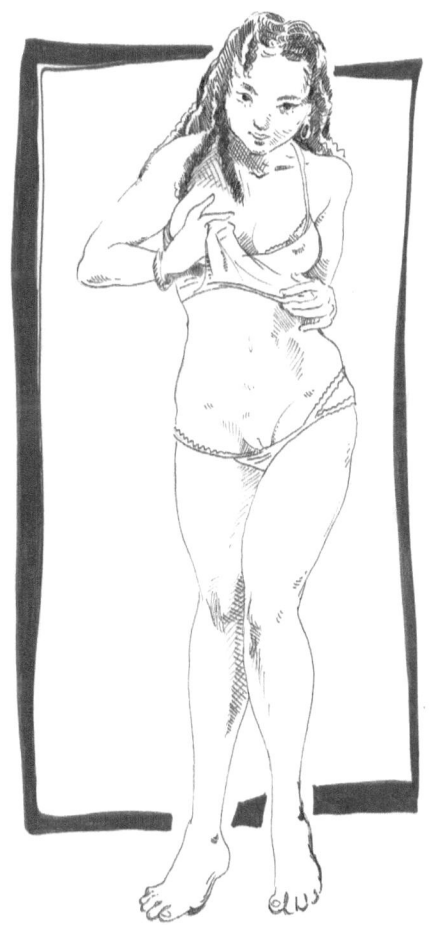

Step 4 - Time to clean my plate. Take you to the shower, lather you up, bathe you and rinse. Towel dry and oil your body. Oh, you thought I was done? No!

Step 5 - I'm still hungry, get on your knees, eat your pussy from the back while I put on my strap, (multitasking is my thing) grab your hips, slide right in, you know how we do from here, can't tell you how you like it...you already know. Fast, slow, in, out, just the tip, deep inside. Moan, scream, call my name, tell me how you feel. Sweat dripping, tears rolling, hair pulling, back scratching. I'm not done yet...oh...wait...you are? Ok...

Skip steps 6-8 for now, jump to Step 9...

Step 9-Cool down, kiss, caress, hold you while you go to sleep. Wanna know what 6-8 were? Wait your turn.

Spring Escapades: WHAT HAPPENS IN VEGAS

Las Vegas in the spring!! Millions come to enjoy the excitement and thrill of the "City of SIN." We came to enjoy a girl's weekend together. You, Autumn, and I decided we needed some fun before Autumn got married in the summer. We chose to stay at "Paris" not only for the ambiance but for the exclusive shopping mall inside the hotel. The view from our suite was phenomenal, overlooking the lights of the strip but also provided extensive landscapes of the desert and mountains in the distance. It made sunset breathtaking from the picture windows of our room. It was by this light that I watched as you and Autumn got undressed to shower and prepare for the night ahead of us. You with your "coke bottle" curves slipped out of your travel clothes and pulled back your hair and with the last article of clothing on the floor, you headed for the large glass door of the huge marble shower. Autumn's tall slender, but shapely body mimicked your every move only she let her long dark wavy hair out of the bun she had it in, shook it loose like one of the women in the "Herbal Essence" commercials, and tiptoed behind you. Rather than take turns, you welcomed her into your warm shower and began to lather one another. It took a few moments before you both noticed that I had moved in closer to watch you play together and at once invited me in for some good, "clean" fun. I accepted the enticing offer and disrobed to join you. The steam from the water only added to the heat of the horseplay which began to take a turn for the erotic when I joined the game. First kissing you deeply and letting my hands grip your hips firmly while Autumn rubbed my back. I found myself working my way down the smooth lines of your body, kissing you slowly until I reached your thighs. You leaned back on the wall of the shower as I raised one of your legs to rest on my shoulder while I kneeled and buried my face to taste you. Autumn took this opportunity to kiss and caress you as you moaned in pleasure and grabbed my hair to maneuver my head where you wanted it. As your legs quivered, I slid you down and let you rest while I turned to partake in Autumn's waiting candy. She chose to lie on the floor of the shower and spread her legs wide apart while I gripped her thighs and

6

indulged myself. Her big green eyes, sparkled as she beckoned for you to come to her. She grabbed your ass as you lowered yourself to her mouth for more of the same treatment I had offered. The steam from the shower made the scene hotter than the most erotic porno movie as we manipulated each other in various positions. The water continued to run all over us and the steam made the sweat "clean" while we continued to please one another. The removable shower head added to the fun as I used it to masturbate while Autumn used her fingers and tongue to please you. Then as if we silently agreed, you and Autumn stood up, I told you both to face the glass as I grabbed you both from behind and played with you as if I were a pianist performing her best piece. The moans from the two of you confirmed my ambidexterity as I brought you both to climax almost simultaneously. As the water cooled and the steam faded, we, one by one, made our way out of the shower. Each refreshed and ready for the evening, we got dressed and prepared for our night on the town. Walking towards the hotel door, each grabbing an arm of the other, we kissed one another and left to take on the "City of Sin," completely and utterly "clean."

Spring Escapades: SOUTHERN HOSPITALITY

Mardi Gras in New Orleans is back and we were there for its return. Excited by the anticipation of the days that lied ahead we arrived to our suite energized and happy. Our hotel was gorgeous; a beautiful replica of an 1800's plantation and our suite was enormous with large windows and glass doors leading to the patio overlooking Bourbon Street. The air was thick with the smell of juniper and lilacs as the room was filled with fresh flowers for our arrival. The room was decorated in the true colors of spring and Carnival, pale yellows and pinks, lavender, and greens, truly welcoming in a Southern yet French fashion and as the bellhop left he summed up the contradicting feeling with a parting "Y'all enjoy your stay, Mademoiselles," a tip of his hat, and a bow farewell. We surveyed the room, taking in the southern charm and then began to unpack and change clothes to go sightseeing. You wore a beautiful white sundress and slides and I chose a jeans skirt and halter top and with a dab of oils for fragrance we were off. The bright sunlight was a warm welcome to the historic city. We walked down the winding brick roads until we came to a wrought iron fence and brick walls around an old cemetery. New Orleans is famous for these burial grounds so we went in to explore. It was late afternoon and the place was deserted so quietly we walked around looking at the old tombstones and wilted flowers. The family crypts truly intrigued us and we ducked inside one to look around. Dusty and dark with very little light from outside peeking in from the tiny windows high around the small room, made it cozy and spooky at the same time. Each nameplate had a small candle above it which made us wonder who maintained these on a daily basis? Each corner had a small chair in it as if set there to let visitors rest and reflect on their memories of their loved ones. It was here we decided to rest for a while.

As you sat in one of the chairs, rays of light from the windows shone on you making your skin glow and your dress practically transparent. Tempted, I moved in and knelt down to kiss you. You responded by kissing me back deeply and wrapping your arms around my neck. We kissed passionately for a while as my hands began to roam your body, rubbing your back as you rubbed mine. Gliding up your legs to your inner thighs, my hands found your moist panties a welcome distraction from their intended path. I let my fingers linger there as you leaned back in the chair while I eased the straps of your sundress off of your shoulders with my mouth. My lips then found their way to your breasts, and I licked and sucked on your nipples while my fingers maneuvered around your panties to dip in your pool of anticipation. My fingers and lips competed for attention and made your legs quiver and my tongue jealous. I put your legs on my shoulders while I slid your panties off and buried my face in the cavern of your pelvis. You ran your hands through my hair and gently pulled taking pleasure in each flick of my tongue and twist of my fingers until finally you pled for me to stop. Hesitantly I did, and with a swift gesture I removed my fingers and licked them for a final taste of your satisfaction as you gasped for breath. You decide fair is fair and tell me to take my place in the chair as you hiked up my skirt and untied my halter to expose my round breasts. You kneeled in front of me with no regard to the dirt floor of the crypt and your white dress and began to suck on my breasts as you skillfully maneuvered my thighs with your hands. As meticulous as a professional painter but as playful as a child with finger paints you dipped your fingers inside me and worked your magic on my body making every nerve tingle with every movement. Faster and deeper you seemed to revel in the sound of my moisture on your fingertips until finally my legs shaking and my stifled screams were a sure sign of my successful journey to ecstasy by way of your hands.

The afternoon sun waned as we dressed and slipped back into the civilized world and made our way to the main road. Dirty, sweaty, and drained, we found our way back to our hotel and up to our suite. We were delighted to see a bath drawn with bubbles and an assortment of bath oils and salts. Big fluffy towels and thick bathrobes hung neatly welcomed us to the end of our first day of vacation. Thankful for the southern hospitality, we bathed and ordered room service and dined by the open windows of our suite. Music from the streets filled the air as the street parade and party began and the smell of Creole food tickled our noses as we marveled at the return of the beautiful, adventure-filled, historic city of New Orleans. We vowed to make this an annual destination, and in answer to the shouts from the street, we threw out the first of many beads to the crowds below.

Spring Escapades: FOLLOW MY DIRECTIONS

Your phone rings, it's the front desk telling you there is a delivery for you. You walk up front to be greeted by a large bouquet of spring flowers with a card attached. A look of bewilderment comes over your face as you read the card which says "Follow My Directions." It has directions to a hotel; instructions on what to wear, what time to arrive and is simply signed "Me." You spend the day confused but excited at what might be in store for you. As your work day ends you rush home to put on your favorite faded blue jeans, and the white button down shirt that look so good together and proceed to follow the directions which guide you to the Doubletree Hotel at Rocky Point on the Causeway. As the valet parks your car you walk into the beautiful lobby of marble floors, mirrored walls, and wood grain accents and are promptly greeted by a friendly concierge off to your right. Smiling broadly at your request for assistance, he directs you to the front desk and states, "This young woman is seeking the room of the person who summoned her here." Smiling sweetly, as if in on a private joke, the clerk hands you a key card and an envelope and directs you to the elevator. You board the elevator heading to the 17th floor, suite 1703 and begin to read the small card enclosed in the envelope. The calligraphy writing details exactly what you should do when you arrive. Step #1: Enter the room, proceed to the bay window, take a glass of champagne, and enjoy the view. You do as instructed and enter the dimly lit room which is impeccably decorated in a modern living room setting in colors of jade green, mauve, and beige. As you approach the window there are strawberries and cheese on a tray next to a single glass of champagne. You sip at the glass, taking in the breathtaking view of the sun setting over the bay. The bright orange and red shades fade to peach, purple and finally dark blue as the sun disappears from the sky. Soft music is playing from the bedroom as you notice the door is now ajar. You enter the room which is only lit by scented candles, dozens of them, all over the room and you are greeted by yet another small envelope, the card enclosed has only one word on it, in large red letters: "STRIP." You let out an uncomfortable laugh at the demanding nature of the note but do as you're told. As you remove the last article of clothing, I enter the room from the bathroom wearing a black bra and panty set with a garter belt, thigh high stockings, and black high heels. In one hand I have a blindfold and in the other, my Japanese bondage ropes. You laugh nervously as I approach you and place the ropes on your wrists, the blindfold on your head, and help you slide up on the bed, and as you lie back on the pillows I place the blindfold over your eyes and place your hands above your head. I pause for a moment to take in your exquisite beauty. Your smooth skin, supple round breasts, and slender body are enticing and I finally begin to partake. With the loss of your sight your other senses are heightened, your body sensitive to my touch as your nose takes in the pungent incense oils burning. Your ears finely tune in to the soft music playing as well as try to determine my next move, as the sound of the whipped cream spraying onto your nipples, neck and pelvic area fills the room. You gasp at the cold substance but are quickly grateful for my hot tongue licking away at the sweet condiment. Your body squirms as I glide my hair across it, you begin to tingle as I kiss and touch you gently so as to arouse your every nerve. Your body is my sensory playground; I spread your legs apart and begin to taste your sweet juices. First slowly and gently so as to taste the savory flavor of your anticipation, then more urgently so as not to waste a drop. My tongue lapping hungrily at your full lips and flicking lightly on your clit, I continue to play, my hands grip firmly on your thighs. You squirm and moan in pleasure as I continue to enjoy your every curve, begging for me to release you, and finally I yield to your request. I remove the blindfold and ropes and let you catch you breath. In a gliding motion you grab me and throw me back on the bed so as to take your turn in control. You meticulously remove my garments one by one being sure to take your time and enjoy yourself. You indulge in pleasuring me in your own special way making sure not to neglect the smallest part of me. With every touch of your hands and lips I quiver in delight. We continue to play our lovers games until the last few candles began to burn low.

Entwined in each other's arms, exhausted from our session we slowly drift off to sleep. You watch as the candles flicker out and wax drips to the floor landing on a familiar piece of paper, the bright red lettering, the last thing you see as you drift off to sleep. A reminder of the night's adventures and the results of simply, following my directions, one word ... "STRIP," you smile and go to sleep.

Spring Escapades: EASTER EGG HUNT

Fresh flowers and budding leaves on the trees were the sure signs that spring was in full bloom as the early morning dew gave the scene a kind of misty coating. I told you I had a special treat for you, wrapped a blindfold around your eyes, and helped you into the car. We drove along the winding road with the windows down as I took you to our favorite park for a special Sunday morning treat. I had hidden colorful eggs throughout the area for you to find for Easter. You shrieked with delight when I removed the blindfold to reveal your spring surprise. There are 3 rules to our game, rule number one, there are 12 colorful eggs hidden for you to find and one golden egg, the golden egg has a secret message inside of it. Rule number two, you can only search in the trees and area around the playground. Finally, rule number three, once the golden egg is found you must do what the message says immediately. You agreed to the rules and ran off to find your treasures. You find the first few eggs easily as they were in plain sight near the bases of various trees and under bushes. Then you find a few more hidden under the slide and the last couple inside the top of the playhouse. Finally its time to search for the golden egg, following the rules, you stick to the designated search area but get frustrated after a while of searching to no avail. Tired, you decide to take a break on the nearest picnic bench; I sat beside you and told you to reach into my jacket pocket where, to your delight, you discovered the golden egg! You open it to find a message inside, "Climb into the playhouse and take off your clothes." You laugh nervously and look at me as I simply say, "Rule number three!" Obediently, you do as you are told and climb up into the playhouse and slowly begin to remove your clothing as I creep in behind you. I lay you down and marvel at your beauty as you eagerly await my plans for you. First, I start by kneeling down and rubbing your feet, working my way up your thighs, feeling you release your tension and anxiousness as I work my way up to your waist. Slowly you begin to relax as I massage you gently from your waistline to across your stomach and up to your chest. I lingered there for a while before moving on to your arms, shoulders and then finally your neck, slowly kissing along the way. It was at this point I produce the final egg for your hunt, the SILVER EGG, vibrator! I turned it on and rolled it over your nipples, down your front to your clit where I let it rest for a moment. You flinched but then grabbed my hand to place it exactly where it provided the most pleasure and moaned and licked your lips at the added sensation until finally you turned your attention back to me. You wrapped your legs around me as I firmly gripped your hips and moved your body to my lap. I could feel your excitement building as your pulse raced upon the first touch of my tongue to your earlobe and as I traced the nape of your neck to your collar bone, chills shot through your body as the special egg's affects lingered. Our breasts pressed against one another, I could feel your heart beat fast and hard as I slid my fingers across your moist clit and rubbed it slowly letting my thumb massage while my forefingers slid inside of you, your moisture now at its peak which made room for more fingers to play. Moving your body to the rhythm of my hips, you rock back and forth on my fingers while I keep a steady grip on your back, your legs wrapping tighter around my back with each movement. My mouth finds your heaving breasts and I suck and lick your nipples never missing the beat of our ride until I can't help but lay you down for a better angle. My fingers worked faster and faster as your moans invited me to keep going deeper. The added pressure of my other hand on your pelvis gave you just the push you needed to go over the edge of ecstasy again and you covered your mouth to stifle your scream. I slowly removed my fingers as you sat up to kiss me passionately almost as if in gratitude. We dressed quickly as it seemed as though the playground had suddenly become inhabited. We climbed down just in time to hear the delighted giggles of the children who had found your discarded colored eggs. You smiled as we walked hand in hand back to the car, your empty golden egg safely tucked in one pocket and the silver egg in the other.

Summer Seduction: *Fire*

I exist to corrupt her pure thoughts of a heterosexual existence.
I cause turmoil in her happy life by being the fuel to her smoldering kindling of past desires for the touch of a woman.
I spark FIRE.

My very presence is a curse of distraction from the mundane tasks of a str8 woman determined to hide her true self from not only the world but herself. She cowers behind false proclamations of sincerity when spewing words denouncing the yearning that is so evident it screams when her mouth is silent.
I spark FIRE.

The longing in her eyes is vaguely veiled by the lust that her touch gives hint to as she desperately tries to deny her needs. One kiss from my lips and she breathes a heavy sigh of relief or is it freedom from her chains of denial. My moist tongue on her breasts and she melts into my waiting arms, the battle is soon done.
I spark FIRE.

My hands on her hips, her body against mine, her fingers dancing in my wet playground, as we venture into the forbidden land of carnal pleasure.
I spark FIRE.

I lick her fingers to consume the essence of pure ecstasy and I bury my head between her thighs to remind her what it feels like to be alive.
I spark a FIRE.

Her hands in my hair and her legs on my shoulders she quivers and moans and lets me know she has been resurrected. Her spirit may have laid dormant buried deep within her soul but to taste life's yearning for even a fleeting moment gives her hope of a reality defined by true acceptance of self.
I spark a FIRE never extinguished.

Summer Seduction: AMAZON VACATION

Hiking through the Amazon jungle was the most creative idea for a vacation you had ever come up with. Our expedition started early in the day with a group of eight including our guide who's expertise had already rubbed off on us. Teaching us plants to beware of and typical hiding spots of treacherous creatures, we felt like true explorers. It was break time and as our group started to disperse for an afternoon snack our guide directed us to pair off and promise to return within one hour. We agreed and ventured off to find our own secluded break area. Although the trees were thick we could still feel the raindrops through the sticky, humid, mist that enveloped the area around us. You looked edible as your skin glistened from the mixture of sweat and rain; the thin white tank top clung to your beautiful curves. The gentle raindrops on your face gave you a glow as your locks curved to your features. I was taken by you in such a way that I couldn't resist kissing you, first on your lips, then cheek, then your neck. I couldn't help but let my hands wonder across your skin, first on your arms, up to your shoulders, then finally across to your soft, supple breasts which I buried my face in and let my tongue run wild. I removed your shirt and laid you back on the blanket we had laid out, careful to beware of strange plants and small creatures. I used your shirt to blindfold you, a technique you loved because it accented your other senses. You giggled and squirmed as I grazed your skin with light touches that sent chills all over while I unbuttoned your shorts. Typically I would also remove your panties but instead I put my warm mouth on the silky material and began to massage your clit until the moisture seeped through the cloth. I continued this while my hands wandered across your smooth skin until I couldn't help but slide my tongue around the material and plunged deep into your well of sweet juices. I lapped hungrily and slid my fingers in and out slowly at first, then faster as your moans told me to proceed. I tried not to neglect your lips as I kissed you deeply still keeping the rhythm of my hands steady as to not break your concentration. Your senses were overwhelmed as the rain fell faster and the waves of pleasure took over your body. Your sweat mixed with rain had you drenched and weak as the final wave took you to climax and you let out a stifled scream so as not to alert the other hikers to our escapade. As we started to dress and gather our belongings, the rain dispersed leaving the heavy mist smelling clean and not so sticky. We rejoined our group smiling and both secretly recounting our break with only one small regret... we were starving! Our entire break was over and we didn't eat anything! (Well...I did!)

Summer Seduction: TRAIN RIDE

You get off from work and the hot Friday traffic in the summer is normally heavy, but for some reason today it seems to be flowing as if it knows you're in a hurry. You arrive at the train station in plenty of time before your train is scheduled to leave. I had already made your reservation and paid for your ticket so all you have to do is find your seat for the short 3 hour ride to Tampa to see me. Looking at your ticket, you board the train and are greeted by a friendly attendant that offers to guide you to your seat. You accept his offer, this being your first time on a train, you are grateful for any assistance. As you walk past the coach and business class seats and through the dining car, you begin to wonder where he is taking you until finally he stops in front of a sleeper car. You are confused because your trip is so short but you go inside anyway. The look of surprise on your face is priceless as you step into the small room and see me standing there smiling at you with a big purple bow around my neck. I'm wearing a short black skirt, tight fitting to show my curves, a low cut v-neck shirt, that accent my cleavage, and thigh high stockings and heels to accentuate my long legs. "What are you doing here!?" you exclaim. "I didn't want your first trip to be alone," I replied, "I flew down to surprise you!" Smiling broadly, you close and lock the compartment door to begin showing your appreciation. You kiss me deeply; your arms wrapped tightly around me and pull me closer, sliding your hands up my back. Your fingertips grazing my skin you begin to "unwrap" your present, untying the bow first, and then removing my shirt. It is then that I took over, pushing you back on the small sleeping bunk and ordering you to sit still and watch. As the train pulled out of the station I turned on the small radio I had brought along and began a slow striptease for you. As I remove my skirt to reveal the garter belt & panties for those sexy thigh highs, you lie back to enjoy the show. My body moved slowly to the beat, my hair swinging across my back had you entranced by my seductive display and after dropping the last piece of my clothing to the floor; I climb on top of you, kissing deeply while my hands maneuver your clothes off of you. This is the last act of control you allow as you turn me over and begin kissing me passionately on my neck and chest, gradually making your way south. Your hands caressing my body as your mouth finds its favorite places to play only stimulates me more until I moan and squirm in pleasure. You kiss me deeply as you plunge your fingers deep inside me over and over again, first slow and sensual, then faster and more urgently taking me from climax to climax but not letting me explode. You continue this erotic torture treatment until I am weak from the overwhelming sensations. Finally it's my turn to return the favor as I flip you over and climb on top of you holding your hands above your head. I slowly glide across your body letting my hair slide along your curves. Gently kissing you from your earlobes to your toes and everywhere in between making sure not to miss a spot, I continue to travel south licking and teasing that sensitive place between your thighs. I let my tongue ring flick on your clit which sends chills through your body. I begin doing that special thing that I do which always makes your body jump so you grab hold of me to try to make me stop. We continue our lover's games taking turns trying to outdo one another until the conductor of the train announces the next stop is Tampa. Reluctantly, we get dressed and prepare to get off, still tingling from our session. As we exit the train, that friendly attendant smiles and says, "Thanks for riding, please come again!" We both look at each other, smile and simultaneously say, "We will!" and walk away both laughing at our private little joke!

Summer Seduction: BOOT CAMP

It is 05:00 as you get dressed for PT, quickly getting into your gear making sure your shoes shine. Just in time to fall in line E3, responding when called, last name only. A frenzy of push ups, mile runs, with sweat dripping, all while dragging your heavy boots. Your face flushed mentally telling yourself you've got to keep up. Meanwhile the Chief Petty officer barking orders at you but still you stand strong. Her being a woman you would think she would understand how hard it is but still she berates you relentlessly. Drills and classes, you are trying to stay focused, working hard to stay ahead. Finally its time to go back to the barracks, time for a shower, you have to clean up in time to eat. The water feels good to you, almost like home, so good that you may have been taking too long, all of your bunkmates are gone. Here comes the Chief Petty officer, yelling at you again, "Fall in line, E3!" Stand at attention in front of your bunk. Chief Petty officer didn't care that you were only in a towel. "Why are you not at chow? Who do you think you are? What makes you so special?" You remind yourself, don't answer, and don't say the wrong thing. She's all in your face, yelling at you but smelling so good. Her deep blue eyes are piercing with anger. Don't do it! Don't give in! It doesn't matter if the Chief Petty officer's uniform fits like it was painted on. You can't look at her like that. "This is the NAVY, and we are the elite," says the Chief Petty officer. "We are well trained, skilled and obedient. Do you understand?" "Yes, Chief Petty officer!" you respond. "Drop that towel E3 and get on your knees." "Yes, Chief Petty officer!" With that command, her pants dropped on the floor and she put her leg on the bunk. (Who knew that Chief Petty officer was a natural blonde?) "Eat my pussy E3 and do it well or you'll be on duty for your next furlough." "Yes, Chief Petty officer!" You grabbed her creamy thighs and licked as if your life depended on it but she tasted so good it was easy to get carried away. Dayum Chief Petty officer please give me some more orders you thought to yourself. "On your feet E3, get behind me." "Yes, Chief Petty officer!" She bent over the bunk and spread her legs. "Fuck me with your fingers E3 and make me come." "Yes, Chief Petty officer"

You did as you were told and did it well, marveling at the Chief Petty officer and how wet she could get. She's silent. Chief Petty officer didn't make a sound while you finger fucked her from the back, fast and hard, finally licking your fingers when you were done. The only indication that you had done your job well was the gasp when you knew she had finally reached her peak and you snatched your fingers back abruptly. "Stand at ease E3" her voice somewhat softer than ever before, almost asking. Chief Petty officer got on her knees and ate your pussy like no one before. Your body wanted to wilt but you were determined to show the same control she did when you made her feel the same way. Her hands were so soft and the way she touched you made your skin tingle. "Look at me E3, did you come?" "Yes, Chief Petty officer!" "As you were, E3 you're late for chow. Get dressed and fall in line. I will expect the same drill tomorrow, same time." She barked orders with a wink as she brushed back her hair into her bun and adjusted her clothes before leaving. "Yes, Chief Petty officer." You respond with a big smile. Military life may not be as bad as you thought. Don't ask, don't tell..

Summer Seduction: HOUSEWARMING

Our new two-story Orlando home is beautiful! It's four bedrooms, four bathrooms, and hardwood floors throughout made all of our months of house hunting worthwhile. The kitchen is huge with cherry wood cabinetry and state of the art, stainless steel appliances. The high ceilings and large bay windows that open out to the salt water pool and Jacuzzi just add to all of the summer sun that the house gets. Most importantly, the Master bedroom with its spacious closets and huge master bath with separate shower and garden tub completed the 1st floor. The 2nd floor loft apartment with media room is an added bonus and makes for a great guest escape.

The furniture is finally all in its place and all of the boxes unpacked and it is time for our first party in our new house. The grill is hot, the beverages are cold, and the kitchen island is covered with side dishes, salads, and fruit. The house is alive with music and chatter as family and friends gather around the pool and living room to catch up with one another. You look amazing in your white two piece swimsuit and matching sheer skirt and with your hair back in a ponytail you look like one of the teenagers in the neighborhood. You winked at me as you took the next tray of food out to the grill. Shortly after, I noticed you slip into the bedroom for what I'm sure was a break from all the festivities and I jumped at the chance to get you alone for a few minutes. I locked the door behind us and grabbed you from behind. You squealed with surprise and giggled at my playfulness when I quickly untied your bikini top and tossed you on the bed.

You slip out of your bikini bottom instinctively for a quick interlude before tending to our guests again. I reached into my nightstand drawer for my favorite dildo to assist me since brevity was required. You straddled the corner of the bed with one leg propped up and I licked you from behind to make sure you were ready for me to play with my friend. I gripped your round behind and spread your cheeks to welcome my accessory. I thrust in slowly and deeply at first but once your Punany recognized the plan she became a slippery path and invited me to go faster. Your leg quivered as I moved with the swiftness of a jackhammer, plunging deep and fast as if trying to force a scream when I knew you were doing all you could to be quiet. You came silently and gripped my hand to let me know you were satisfied and ready to take a break from your "break." I complied and went to put away my toy while you, not wanting to wear panties anymore, slipped into a sundress. I praised your choice for it warranted me an opportunity to touch you at any time during the evening. You smiled mischievously and replied, "I know." The night went on and periodically I would catch you behind a counter or in the kitchen alone, lift your skirt, and get on my knees to taste you. It became a game to see how long we could get away with it until someone came in at which point I would act as though I had just dropped something and stand up. This worked well until the one time I got carried away with you sitting at the table while I was under it. We didn't hear my sister come in the kitchen and your sister come in from the pool at the same time. I couldn't get up without being detected so I stayed quiet. Unfortunately for you but fortunate for me, they sat down to have a conversation.

I couldn't resist the chance to see if you could keep your composure while they spoke of their lives, children, and jobs while I continued to spread your legs under the table and stick my tongue and fingers deep inside you. I have to give you credit, you did well at first, only taking a deep breath at times but still wrapping your legs around my neck and pulling me closer, but then occasionally you had to "adjust your seat." After a while I decided to put more pressure on you to see if you would try to clear the room, so I started to suck hard on your clit while fingering you faster and you jumped in your seat. Thinking quickly you explained that you thought a bug was on your leg but when they offered to check you told then it was just your dress and not to bother. Unable to take much more you asked the ladies to check on the party guests at the pool while you go freshen up. They do so, and as they walk out, you grab me out from under the table laughing at how unfair this particular game was.

I ran out to the pool where I could safely escape punishment and stood amongst friends just out of your reach. You shake a warning finger to let me know that retaliation was inevitable. The sun began to set over the lake behind our house and as you walked the last guests to the door, I gathered up the remnants of a great pool party. The grill is cleaned off, the cups and plates discarded, and all that is left is to pick up the random pool floats and put them away. I turned to reach for the last raft in the pool when all of the sudden you run up behind me and pushed me in! Fully dressed and in complete shock I gasped for air asking, "What was that for?!" You strip down out of your dress and smile coyly as you walk towards me, "Its time for payback!" and with that you jumped into the pool and swam to me wrapping your arms around my neck. I removed my clothes and as the evening sky turned to night I took my "punishment" for the next 2 hours until finally our wrinkled, tired, bodies got out of the pool and into our bed. Thoroughly spent we dozed off to sleep, in our bed, in the master bedroom, of our four bedroom, four bath, dream home.

Fall Fantasies: *Tell Me Your Fantasy*

Tell me your fantasy baby...whisper to me.
I won't tell anyone...

Tell me how you want to be whisked away to a deserted island, and made love to on the soft white beach, while the deep blue waves crash over our bodies...

Tell me your fantasy baby...whisper to me.
I won't tell anyone...

Tell me how when you're at work chained to your computer, you picture me there, under your desk, licking your pussy, while your boss walks by to ask for that report...

Tell me your fantasy baby...whisper to me.
My lips are sealed...

Tell me how you want to go in the dressing room of Frederick's to try on lingerie and how you want me to rip it off you, put your face against the mirror and finger fuck you while you try to be quiet...

Tell me your fantasy baby...whisper in my ear.
Tell me how you want me to tie your legs apart, handcuff your wrists, blindfold you, lay you on your stomach and fuck you till your screams can be heard by the elderly couple down the street with their hearing aids OFF!

Tell me your fantasy baby...whisper softly to me.
Tell me what you want me to hear. Tell me that you come here secretly waiting for me to take you to the bathroom, close the stall door, sit you on the counter and do all the things your boyfriend you came here with won't do, and do them WELL!

Tell me your fantasy baby...I'm talking to you. When you walk into that restaurant and the long table cloths make you think of how I'm going to be under them sucking your toes, licking your thighs, and licking your clit...

Tell me your fantasy baby...your secret is safe with me.
Tell me you want to know what its like to be on stage with Immani Love while she acts out each and every one of her poems and bedtime stories one by one, slowly and on camera.
Come on baby, tell me your fantasy. Whisper to me. I won't tell a soul.
Unless...you want me to.

Fall Fantasies: STROLL IN THE PARK

Fall evening skies with its shades of orange, red, blue and purple cover the trees of the park I like to visit. The squeaky wooden walkway leads deep into the woods along side the murky lake that the park is named after. You and I walk hand and hand along the trail, quietly taking in the scenery. Wild birds flying overhead and the rippling water below remind us that we are guests in this playground for nature's residents. Our thoughts are confirmed as we watch a gator slip into the water from the far banks of the lake. It's a warm night with a gentle breeze as dusk makes its descent into darkness. Our trail lit only by scattered lampposts and moonlight, we make our way to one of the many benches overlooking the water. You look sexy and comfortable in your faded jeans and button down shirt and I am stunning as usual with a jeans mini skirt to show off my long brown legs and a sheer, backless, halter top accenting my smooth skin.

As you sit on the bench and look at me, I lean on the rail in front of you looking out onto the calm water, my hair gently blowing in the breeze. I turn to look at you and smile that seductive smile that makes you wonder what I'll do next. Before you can speak, I untie the halter of my shirt and let it drop to the ground revealing my supple breasts and walk towards you. I straddle your lap and begin to unbutton your shirt as you lean back and smile as you decide to see how far I'll go. I take off your shirt and remove the "wife beater" beneath to leave only your sports bra between my mouth and your breasts. I begin to nibble on your neck and make my way to your chest as your hands caress my back rubbing up and down and finally sliding around to cup my breasts and play with my firm nipples. As I make my way back up to your neck, you turn the tables on me and slide out from under me and put me on the bench. You kneel down and in front of me and glide your hands up my legs, slowly making your way to the moist place between my thighs. You let your fingers dance in their playground while I squirm and moan in pleasure and try to pull you closer, my hands entangled in your hair. Just when I think you are easing up to let me catch my breath, you bury your face deep between my legs, hiking up my skirt so as to spread my limbs further apart. You plunge your tongue deep into my treasure chest as I wrap my legs around your neck and throw my head back enveloped in the waves of electricity going through my body with every flick of your tongue. You continue to bring me to the brink of climax and stop me just shy of explosion over and over again, teasing me with the taste of ecstasy only to rob me of it for a few moments longer until I'm begging you for mercy. Finally, you give in to my pleading sighs and allow me to have the moment of elation I had been pleasantly tortured trying to achieve.

As I melt into your arms, chills running through me, you put your shirt over me to help tame the combination of shivering and goose bumps that overwhelmed my body. You gently kiss my lips with the passion of the moments before then bend down to gather the rest of our clothes. As we walk back towards the exit, you grab my hand and smile as if to say what we both know to be true…when we get home, ROUND II!

Fall Fantasies: INTRUDER

I'm getting home from work, dusk taking over the sky, shades of dark blue and orange crease the sky as the summer sun begins to set. I walked into our home, not wanting to turn on lights, letting the skylights allow sunset to light my way to our bedroom. The giant picture window allows optimal view from our king sized canopy bed and through the dainty sheers the last light of day fades away. I turn on some slow music to unwind as I hang up the phone. You had called to tell me you are working a little late and not to wait up so I lie across the bed and close my eyes to take in the mood. I didn't hear the intruder come into the room; I didn't have a chance to scream as I was grabbed. I was overtaken, my mouth covered, my eyes blindfolded and with great force I was thrown on the bed and tied to the corners. I couldn't move, I couldn't fight and my silent attacker meticulously undressed me. First my blouse ripped open and my bra snatched apart, then my skirt hiked up and my panties ripped off of me. Fear gripped my body as thoughts of you run through my mind. Where are you? Why aren't you here to help me? Who is this and why are they doing this to me? As the tears well up in my eyes I can feel my assailants breath close to my skin. First, my neck, smelling my hair, then against my breasts, pausing for a moment before moving south to my pelvic area, between my thighs nearing the place that belongs to only you. As my heart races, my mind reels trying to think of a way to break free. Just when I can't bear the terror any longer, I hear the voice. At first drowned out by my thoughts, and then becoming clearer until finally unmistakably recognizable! I know who this is, and as my senses once overwrought with fear, now subside with familiarity, the words spoken to me ring clear. "I'm here, baby, relax." You gently wipe away my tears of fear and kiss my cheeks as you remove my blindfold and uncover my mouth. You untied me and I grab you and wrap my arms around your neck burying my face close to you as you calmly lay me back onto the bed. I am consumed by the extreme emotions overtaking me as you begin to touch me gently, sending chills down my spine.

Your lips are now a welcome treat as you kiss me deeply and passionately before beginning your journey south. Your tongue is gliding down my body, flicking quickly across my skin, finally reaching the most sensitive place to play. You linger there lapping hungrily at my juices as I call your name and running my fingers through your hair. Engulfed in the waves of ecstasy you provide I finally reach the moment I have been consumed by trying to achieve. I melted back onto the bed bereft of any energy in my body. Drained of all emotions and trembling from the traumatic experience of the evening, I lay motionless; you lie beside me, holding me close and speaking softly into my ear. As I drift off to sleep, your comforting words a constant reminder of what I already know to be true. "I love you, baby, and no matter where you are, what you do, and whatever happens, I am always with you, now and forever." And with that we fall asleep entwined in each others arms.

Fall Fantasies: TWINS

I love to visit you at your house the exquisite designs and color schemes are pleasing to the eye from the golden leaf accents in the living and dining areas to the West Indies palm trees in the bathroom. I especially like the four-poster beds with their tall wooden posts, which seem as though they were made for my imagination to go wild. I walked into your room unlike your sister's jungle paradise you have a distinct zebra like motif complete with the black and white zebra skin rug. I turn off your lights leaving it dark with the exception of the zebra night light I bought you and the candles that match the décor. I too, blend very well with the aura tonight. I'm wearing a black dress with Japanese hooks outlined with white seams, black thigh high stockings and high heels. The dress hugs my curves and the dim light of the candles casts a sexy silhouette on the wall. You, knowing full well my intentions, turn on one of your slow mix cds that always make me wet and you lie back on the bed and watch me as I begin my personal striptease for you. As I dance, you glance your eyes over my body as I ask you to unzip my dress to reveal the black lace bra and garter with crotch-less panties (a Frederick's original.) By now you are so aroused you begin removing your clothes as I climb on the bed and crawl towards you, crawling on top you pushing you back to lie down. I pull your blindfold from under your pillow and place it over your eyes and the four silk scarves I keep at your house to tie your arms and legs apart. While I'm tying you up my pussy is over your face as a sweet tease just out of your tongue's reach. I slide back down your body, pausing to kiss and lick your neck and breasts. While I take pleasure in kissing you all over your chest, my body rubs against yours to the beat of the music. As I grind on you I slip my fingers down to feel your wet lips and proceed to play in your playground with my fingers making you squirm with my every touch. My fingers dripping wet with your juices I can't help but lick them careful not to waste a drop of your nectar. You taste so good I have to slide down and sample you firsthand, my tongue flicking across your lips then deep inside your pool of delight. In and out, over and over until you moan in pleasure I continue licking your lips and clit until I feel you trying to wiggle free from your bonds. I take great pleasure in licking and sucking on your clit while my fingers wander around inside you. First slow and sensual, then faster, the closer you come to your first climax. Not yet! The abrupt stopping of the sensation sends you into a frustrated frenzy so I untie you but instruct you to let me finish while you grasp my hair pulling it whenever I hit a good spot until you can't take anymore and I finally let you explode. At which point you grab me throw me down on the bed and tell me that payback is a bitch and it's my turn to suffer. You place the blindfold on me and tie me up making sure to strip me naked for full access to my body.   You proceed to give me a similar treatment only with your own personal touch. You begin to do things to me that I had only imagined possible! From your tongue, to the skillful way your fingers manipulate my body, to the various toys you torture and tease me with. I reached so many levels of ecstasy with you I was in tears from being overwhelmed by my multiple orgasms. After several hours of pleasing each other we both were exhausted from trying to outdo the other and we just lay back on the bed in each other's arms, smiling as we close our eyes both silently thinking to ourselves. The same thing...I am hungry! Who's going to cook?

Winter Warmth: *"Morning Routine"*

Sunlight graces my yellow walls and its morning again. It's 6:30am, Time for my morning routine.

Alarm goes off, I turn it off. I turn to my right, Yup, she's still asleep.
Reach under the covers,
Yup, she's got those boy shorts on.
6:34am, Yup, time to
"wake and taste."
Roll over to her side of the bed. She feels me near her. Reach down to rub her legs, they spread to welcome me. My hand on her short feeling her through the cotton,
Yup, she's wet. Massage her lit, Yup, she's moving with me. 6:42am,
Yup, time to remove yet another pair of ruined shorts.
"Good morning, naked!" "Good morning, beautiful!"
I bury my face in her wet pussy, licking, sucking, rubbing.
She's talking to me, that pussy,
Yup, "slide your fingers in, Mani, I'm ready for you."
Damn that pussy be talking shy to me!
"Ok, if you insist!" Yup it's a two finger morning.
In and out, fast and slow, don't you just love that sound? You know the one, the "wet pussy on my fingers" sound.
Yup, she's wide awake now, breathing heavy, pulling my hair, sweating.
Still licking`and sticking, fingers moving faster now,
deeper now, changing angles now.
Yup, her breasts need to be sucked now; her neck needs to be kissed now her lips, OH, her LIPS! Still feeling her she's quivering now, muscles flexing, gripping my fingers now. Legs clamped on my neck now. Yup, gotta lick the rest of those juices now. Clean up time! Oooh look at my fingers!
Yup, gotta lick them too! 8:06am DAYUM, late for work again!
Love my morning routine,
YUP!

Winter Warmth: DINNER DATE

The décor of the restaurant I chose was cozy and romantic. Dark burgundy walls with black and gold accents, each table draped with long black tablecloths, fresh flowers and burgundy cloth napkins with gold rings around them. The high backs of the booths allowed for a feeling of seclusion and privacy. Our server started our meal with a bottle of Sangria and two chilled glasses. We lingered over our drinks sitting across from one another, conversing about our day and taking in the other's company.

As our dinner salads arrived our conversation turned more intense and I moved by your side to be able to whisper in your ear. I leaned in close with one hand tucking your hair back, my lips close to your ear and my other hand gliding up your thigh. As I whispered my intentions, you laughed nervously and looked into my eyes to see if I was serious. "I'm going to finger you before our main course and then YOU will be my dessert." I said. I stared intently into your eyes to show you I wasn't joking as I slid my hand up and down your leg. I moved my fingers slowly up to my mouth, licked them and then gently traced the soft flesh of your inner thigh and slowly upward until I reached my prize. You were moist with anticipation and I could feel the heat from your sweet cavern through your panties. First, I traced the outline of your "lips" enjoying the sticky moisture that glossed them. My forefinger found your jeweled treasure and I lingered there long enough to watch you lick your lips in pleasure. Then with one swift motion I slipped my fingers deep inside your well and you gasped and grabbed my hand. At first, because of the abrupt movement but then to maneuver it to where you wanted it.

I massaged your clit as I glided my fingers in and out feeling the moisture between them until your thighs tensed to let me know you were fulfilled for now. Our timing was perfect as our server came with our main course. We dined leisurely and talked as if nothing had happened. It seemed as though I wouldn't follow through on my earlier statement by the way our conversation progressed. I finished before you and waited while you ate and looked at the dessert menu. You ordered your dessert and proceeded to finish your meal. You glanced down for a moment and with a swift unnoticed movement I was under the long table cloth before you could look up again, steadily licking up your thigh. You jumped, startled by my aggressive maneuver but then as I buried my head deeper you leaned back to enjoy MY dessert.. The waiter came back with your crème brulee and you composed yourself well enough to thank him as I continued to indulge in my sweet treat. He asked if I would be having anything for dessert and you replied with a gasp as I inserted my fingers, « I think she's having some of mine ! » You gripped the table tightly as the waiter knowingly winked, smiled, and walked away. After some time, I finished my candy and joined you at the table just in time to pay the check and bid our friendly, discreet waiter farewell. As we walked to the car, you grabbed my hand, licked my fingers, and sweetly told me what I already knew....when we got home; it was time for your midnight snack!

Winter Warmth: WAKE UP CALL

You're sleeping peacefully beside me, your arm gently draped around me. It's 3am and I'm wide awake! I turn to look at you and decide to wake you the way only I can. First, gently kissing your lips, forehead, and eyelids until you open your eyes. Then, before you can speak, kiss you deeply and passionately so as not to leave a question in your mind as to my intentions. I place my body on top of yours while my kiss moves slowly from your lips to your neck and collarbone, arousing the sensuality within you as you respond by squeezing me tightly. You glide your hands across my nude body as you grip my hips and pull me closer to you. I lay across your chest looking into your beautiful eyes, taking in all the love and passion I see in them before I sit up to take your pleasure tool into my wet, well of lust. I wind my hips, slowly at first, while you caress my thighs. As my movements quicken you sit up to hold me close and feel yourself deeper inside me. With this action, I wrap my long legs around your back and lock them together, never missing a beat of my stroke while I kiss you passionately making sure you taste my love in every way. You bury your face in my round breasts licking and sucking and my firm nipples respond accordingly. You grip my back whispering in my ear how much you love me and I respond by thrusting my hips deeply towards you just to remind you one of the reasons why! I lift one leg up in front of you as I turn around, never letting our bodies lose their connection as I am now sitting with my back to you, I motion for you to lie back and enjoy the ride. Moving up and down, in and out, slowly teasing you with quick and abrupt maneuvers, I bring you to the verge of climax only to stop you just before you can savor the moment. Now trying to gain control, you lean me over the edge of the bed with my body arched over a pillow while you grasp my shoulders and thrust your "manhood" deep inside me, slowly at first, then faster as I scream your name and tell you to fuck me harder. You continue the rhythm with one hand on my shoulder and the other playing with my clit as I moan in delight. You toss my overwhelmed body onto the bed on my back and grab my legs as you lean in to taste the fruits of your labor. My hips rotate to ride your tongue as you lap away at your "just dessert." I grab your hair and pull you close to me and invite you to slide inside me to feel the slippery treat you deserve. My moist cavern is a familiar feeling and my body responds to you as an old friend welcomes its mate. As I wrap and lock my legs around your back once again you can no longer hold back and finally give in to ecstasy. Sweating and breathless, you hold me in your arms and say, glancing at the clock, "Damn woman! You sure know how to give a great wake up call, it's 6am!!! What a way to start the day!"

Winter Warmth: CABIN FEVER

Wooded, romantic, seclusion was the goal when we decided to go camping for the weekend. Our novice attempt at "roughing it" would teach us just how much we really knew about the outdoors. The temperature was unseasonably cold for a Georgia winter but it made for perfect snuggling weather and the state park we chose had charming, rustic cabins for us to bunk in. Our four room cabin consisted of the living room with fireplace, which was decorated with all the great outdoors had to offer in wildlife taxidermy complete with bear skin rug and fireplace fully stocked with firewood. A long couch and a recliner strategically placed in front of the over sized hearth made it evident that this would be our main means of entertainment. The small kitchen doubled as a dining area, and the bathroom boasted an old fashioned claw foot tub. The bedroom was cozy; it was dimly lit on both sides of the bed by traditional oil lanterns set on small nightstands and a large oil lamp on the rickety old dresser, the mirror used to help amplify its light. A large handmade quilt draped over the end of the bed and a woven rug at the foot, completed the look. We felt like true pioneers as we unpacked our belongings and began to prepare for our evening in the "wilderness." It was a quiet, clear night and although it was cold, we bundled up and took a blanket outside to lie under the stars, silently taking in the natural beauty of the dense woodlands and listening to the various sounds of its animal inhabitants. We held each other tightly to increase our body heat until finally we decided that the perfectly good fireplace INSIDE was the best option for optimal warmth as the snow flurries began to dust the area. Slightly damp from the snow, we stripped down in front of the fireplace that was, by this time, at full blaze. I hadn't noticed until just then how rosy your cheeks were and the moisture on your face gave you a radiant glow in front of the fire. Your nude body became all the more enticing as you knelt down on the fluffy, bear skinned rug to get closer to the heat. It was at that moment I knew I had to have you. I moved closer to you and knelt behind you with my arms around you pressing my breasts close to your back. My hands found their familiar place cupping your round, firm breasts and slightly pinching your nipples gently between my fingers. My breath was hot on the back of your neck as I breathed in the sweet smell of your hair while I nibbled on your shoulders. You lean back onto the rug as if instinctively following my lead, as I move in front of you to put my lips on your now firm nipples and suck gently while I lightly bite the way you like. My hands were roaming your body until they found your hips slightly raised to meet mine. I climbed on top of you pressing my hips against yours, our legs between each other and our pelvises matched. We moved in a rhythm of the crackling fire and our racing heartbeats in unison. Faster and harder until the moisture of our anticipation was beginning to wet our legs and our sweat began matting the fur of our silent companion. I couldn't wait any longer, I had to taste you! I swiftly dove between your thighs and dug my tongue deep into the pool of desire that awaited me, cupping my tongue like a spoon so as not to miss a drop. I propped your legs on my shoulders and gripped your thighs while you pulled my hair to show your approval of my new position. My tongue and long fingers took turns dipping into your pool until finally you let out a scream of climax that made coyote outside howl with you. With that I pulled you close to me and you laid on my chest as we watched the dying embers of the fire glow until we dozed off to sleep. We awoke in the morning to the chill of the now dark fireplace and the white windows which were covered by snow. We were snowed in! You chuckled at my concern and simply said, no worries, we still have three more rooms to "warm up.

OUTRO: ADDICTED

This is a public service announcement. Hi, my name is Immani Love, and I'm addicted to pussy.

I'm a punany fiend, a carpet munching fool; I will get on my knees and beg for a hit of that shyt that makes me high. I'm hooked and I don't want to be cured.

I'm the best kind of addict to have around cuz my addiction has very few side effects. I can take hit after hit, after hit, and the only down side is ... that damn pussy might go to sleep!

My affliction is diverse too; I can get it in all forms just like any drug on the street. I like tall pussy, short pussy, fuzzy pussy, shaved pussy, jeweled pussy, wet pussy, just as long as it's CLEAN pussy!

I can sniff it, lick it, swallow it, and if I'm good I can keep a constant supply of it.

But I'm the worst kind of addict too, cuz when I don't have enough of it I might steal yours.

And once I get hold of it, I will kiss it, lick it, suck it in ways you've never imagined and now what used to be your pussy is an addict too, it's addicted to ME.

It wants hit after hit after hit and before you know it that damn pussy is on her knees begging for a hit of that shyt that made her high.

It's a vicious cycle.

This is a public service announcement. Beware of that snatch, that crotch, that candy, that sweet sticky treat that makes men and women alike go weak.

I'm addicted to pussy. Hi, my name is Immani Love.

www.ingramcontent.com/pod-product-compliance
Lightning Source LLC
Chambersburg PA
CBHW031330290526
45784CB00014B/2540